YOUR BREATHTAKING LUNGS

and

 ROCKING

Respiratory System

FIND OUT HOW YOUR BODY WORKS!

Paul Mason

Crabtree Publishing Company

www.crabtreebooks.com

Crabtree Publishing Company
www.crabtreebooks.com
1-800-387-7650

Published in Canada
Crabtree Publishing
616 Welland Avenue
St. Catharines, ON
L2M 5V6

Published in the United States
Crabtree Publishing
PMB 59051
350 Fifth Ave, 59th Floor
New York, NY 10118

Author: Paul Mason
Editorial director: Kathy Middleton
Editors: Annabel Stones, Shirley Duke, Kelly Spence
Designer: Rocket Design (East Anglia) Ltd
Consultant: John Clancy, Former Senior
    Lecturer in Applied Human Physiology
Proofreaders: Susie Brooks, Rebecca Sjonger
Prepress technician: Margaret Amy Salter
Print and production coordinator: Margaret Amy Salter

Published by Crabtree Publishing Company in 2016

First published in 2015 by Wayland
Copyright © Wayland, 2015

Picture credits:
Getty Images: p4 Barcroft Media / contributor, p9 bl Mike Powell / staff, p13 b Samo Vidic / contributor, p22 William Radcliffe, p25 r Chiaki Nozu / contributor; iStockphoto: p19 cl FangXiaNuo; Mary Evans: p21 cl Mary Evans Picture Library; Science Photo Library: 9 tl ALFRED PASIEKA, p10 D. PHILLIPS, p23 tl EDDY GRAY; Shutterstock: Cover, p3 cr, p3 b, p5 bl, p6, p7 br, p12, p14 bl, p14 br, p15 bl, p15 br, p16, p17 tr, p17 br, p18, p19 tr Joe Seer, p20, p21 tr, p21br, p23 bl, p24, p25 t, p26, p27 tr, p27 br TonyV3112, p28 l, p28 br, p29 t, p29 c, p29 bc. CC Wikimedia Commons: p11 b. Graphic elements from Shutterstock.

Artwork: Ian Thompson: p5 r, p8; Stefan Chabluk: p3 t, p7 c, p9 br, p11 t, p13 t, p19 br.

Printed in the USA/082015/SN20150529

Library and Archives Canada Cataloguing in Publication

Mason, Paul, 1967-, author
    Your breathtaking lungs and rocking respiratory system / Paul Mason.

(Your brilliant body!)
Includes index.
Issued in print and electronic formats.
ISBN 978-0-7787-2195-6 (bound).--ISBN 978-0-7787-2209-0 (paperback).--
ISBN 978-1-4271-1706-9 (pdf).--ISBN 978-1-4271-1700-7 (html)

    1. Respiratory organs--Juvenile literature. 2. Lungs--Juvenile literature.
I. Title.

QM251.M37 2015   j612.2   C2015-903165-6
                                                            C2015-903166-4

Library of Congress Cataloging-in-Publication Data

Mason, Paul, 1967-
 Your breathtaking lungs and rocking respiratory system / Paul Mason.
    pages cm. -- (Your brilliant body!)
 Includes index.
 ISBN 978-0-7787-2195-6 (reinforced library binding : alk. paper) --
ISBN 978-0-7787-2209-0 (pbk. : alk. paper) --
ISBN 978-1-4271-1706-9 (electronic pdf : alk. paper) --
 ISBN 978-1-4271-1700-7 (electronic html : alk. paper)
1. Respiration--Juvenile literature. 2. Lungs--Physiology--Juvenile literature.
I. Title.

QP121.M376 2016
612.2--dc23
                                        2015015359

CONTENTS

Cells are the smallest building blocks of all living things.

Lots of cells join together to make tissue. Tissue forms the thin linings, or membranes, within the lungs.

Your lungs are the main organs in your respiratory system. They are made of many different types of cells and tissue.

The lungs work with other organs in your respiratory system to allow you to take air in and push it out of your body.

YOUR BREATHTAKING LUNGS

Every minute, you breathe in about 15 times—even more if you are exercising. The air you breathe in travels through roughly 1,243 miles (2,000 km) of **airways**—passages that carry air deep into your lungs. It's an impressive set up… but what is it for?

Why do I breathe?

You breathe to get air in and out of microscopic air sacs within your lungs. From the outside, a healthy lung looks pink and spongy. You have two lungs, one on each side of your chest. They are surrounded by rows of bones, called ribs. These form a protective barrier called your **rib cage**.

Air contains a mixture of gases. About 20% of air consists of a gas called **oxygen**. You need a constant supply of oxygen to stay alive. Your brain, liver, heart, and other organs and muscles all need oxygen. You can survive for days without water, and weeks without food—but you would last only a few minutes without oxygen.

Many mountain climbers carry breathing equipment containing oxygen. The higher you climb, the less oxygen there is in the air.

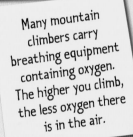

When the air you breathe in reaches your lungs, the oxygen is removed and absorbed into your blood, ready to be distributed around the rest of your body. Oxygen is used to release energy from the food you eat. This energy is needed by every part of your body to keep it working.

You need to breathe for another reason, too. Getting energy from food creates a waste gas called **carbon dioxide**. Breathing out rids your body of this gas.

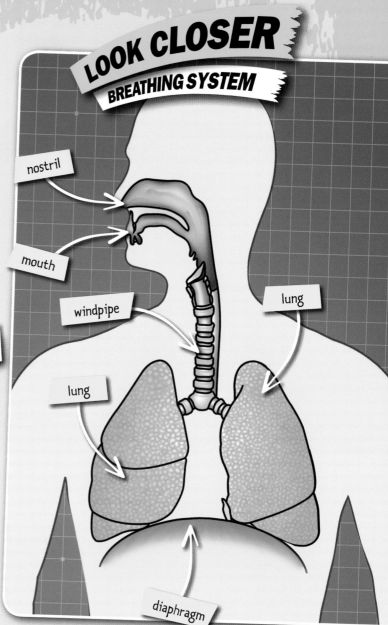

LOOK CLOSER
BREATHING SYSTEM

nostril

mouth

windpipe

lung

lung

diaphragm

DON'T TRY THIS AT HOME!

Most people can go without breathing for between 20 and 45 seconds. After specialist training, some people can hold their breath for MUCH longer than that. In 2012, **freediver** Stig Severinsen set a world record by holding his breath underwater for 22 MINUTES!

Holding your breath for a long time without training is dangerous, so really DON'T try this at home.

Freedivers dive down to great depths without the use of breathing equipment.

STRANGE BUT TRUE!

Babies start life taking 40 to 50 breaths per minute. By the time they are five or six years old, the number of breaths they take per minute is only about 15. That's the same as an adult.

NOSTRILS AND MOUTH

Your nose and mouth are the starting point for your respiratory system, where air is drawn in. They are also the security guards—part of their job is to stop anything getting in that shouldn't be there.

BRILLIANT BODY FACT

Your nose warms cold air (or cools hot air) as you breathe in!

Keeping out intruders

A constant supply of air reaching your lungs is needed to keep you alive. You don't really want anything else getting into your lungs, though. It could damage the airways, or the lungs themselves. Your body takes defensive measures to keep out any unwelcome guests.

The hairy snot trap

One way unwelcome guests could get into your respiratory system is through your nostrils.

Hairs in your nostrils trap dirt and germs—two of the three main ingredients of slimy snot. (The other one is **mucus**—sticky stuff from further up your nostrils.). Snot may also contain **microbes** that can make you sick.

Further inside the **nasal passages** are microscopic hairs called **cilia**. These are coated with sticky mucus, which trap any leftover dirt and microbes. The cilia are constantly moving. As they do this, they move the mucus, dirt, and germs out of your nasal passages.

Cilia are your nose's clean-up crew.

Pieces of food

You use your mouth not only for breathing, but also for eating. But getting food in your lungs would be a really bad idea! To stop this from happening, you have an **epiglottis**. The epiglottis is a leaf-shaped flap of skin that changes its position, depending on whether you are breathing or swallowing. Normally, the epiglottis is open, which allows you to breathe. When you swallow food or liquids, the flap closes and prevents anything from getting into your lungs.

LOOK CLOSER
THE EPIGLOTTIS

The epiglottis is open for breathing.

The epiglottis closes when you swallow.

air

mouth

epiglottis

mouth

food pipe

epiglottis

food pipe

windpipe

windpipe

DID YOU KNOW?

Horses can't breathe through their mouths.

Horses can only breathe through their nostrils. A flap of tissue forms a tight seal at the back of the mouth, sealing it off from the throat. The flap only opens when the horse wants to swallow food or water.

JOURNEY TO THE LUNGS

At first, the air you breathe and the food you eat share an entry passage into your body—the throat, or **pharynx**. Soon, though, the air enters its own tube called the **trachea**. This leads to a maze of passageways that take air into the lungs.

Trachea and bronchi

After you breathe it in, air goes past the epiglottis (see page 7) and is pulled into the trachea, which is also known as the "windpipe." Like parts of your nose, the trachea is lined with cilia. The cilia trap and expel dirt and germs.

Next, the trachea divides into two **bronchi**, carrying air toward either your left or right lung. The bronchi divide, so that they can deliver air to different parts of your lungs. You might think that's it— the air has passed along the bronchi and is in your lungs—great! But the air isn't at the end of its journey yet.

LOOK CLOSER
INSIDE THE LUNGS

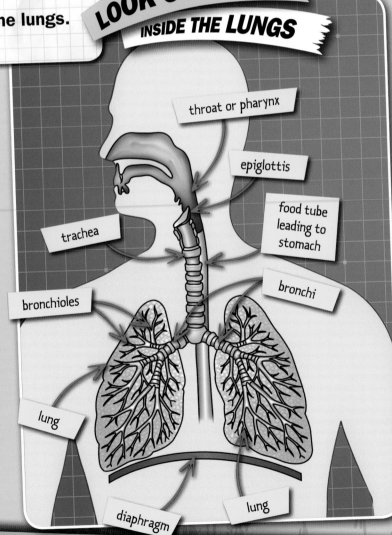

throat or pharynx

epiglottis

food tube leading to stomach

trachea

bronchi

bronchioles

lung

lung

diaphragm

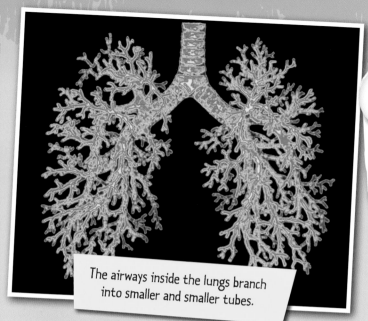

The airways inside the lungs branch into smaller and smaller tubes.

The bronchioles

The bronchi feed air into smaller tubes called **bronchioles**. The bronchioles split again and again, so that the whole of your lung is lined with a network of tiny air passages. The smallest are only as thin as thread. They are so tiny that there's room for about 30,000 of them in EACH LUNG!

See for yourself

Find out how much air your lungs hold!

Take a large, empty drink bottle and fill it with water. Fill a plastic bowl halfway with water. Cover the end of the bottle, so that no water spills out, then turn the bottle upside down in the bowl, and uncover the end.

Take a bendable straw and put the short section into the opening of the bottle under the water. Let the longer end stick up out of the water.

Take a deep breath, and blow into the long end of the straw for as long as you can.

The amount of air in the bottle is the amount that was in your lungs!

DID YOU KNOW?

Your lungs are different sizes.

Not only are your lungs slightly different sizes, they also have different structures. The right lung is bigger and has three **lobes**. The left lung is smaller and has only two lobes.

The difference is because your heart tilts to the left, so it takes up more space on the left side of your chest.

STRANGE BUT TRUE!

Most adults can hold a maximum of about 1.3 gallons (5 L) of air in their lungs—but there are exceptions. The Spanish cyclist Miguel Indurain had amazingly large, 2.1 gallon (8 L) lungs. Indurain's lungs were SO big that they pushed his stomach down and outward.

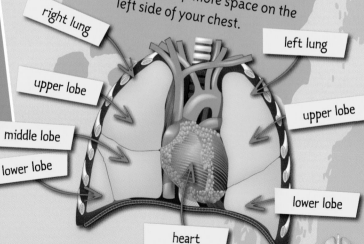

right lung

left lung

upper lobe

upper lobe

middle lobe

lower lobe

lower lobe

heart

THE ALVEOLUS
OXYGEN EXCHANGE

The lungs are your only organs that would float, if removed. They can do this because they contain millions of miniature air sacs, called **alveoli**. Each alveolus (the name for just one of the air sacs) contains only a tiny amount of air—but you have a LOT of them. Together they hold enough air to keep the lungs afloat.

BRILLIANT BODY FACT

Your lungs work SO well, you can survive with only one!

Amazing alveoli

At the end of the tiniest bronchioles in each lung are the alveoli. You have about 600 million alveoli altogether! That's so many in total that if they were all spread out flat on the ground, you could easily cover a tennis court with them.

Wrapped around each alveolus are tiny **blood vessels** called **capillaries**. These are SO tiny that blood cells have to pass through them one at a

tissue

red blood cells

capillary wall

Red blood cells pass one at a time through a tiny capillary.

time. Between the alveolus and the capillary is a **membrane** just one cell thick. This is so thin that 50 of them on top of one another would only be as thick as tissue paper.

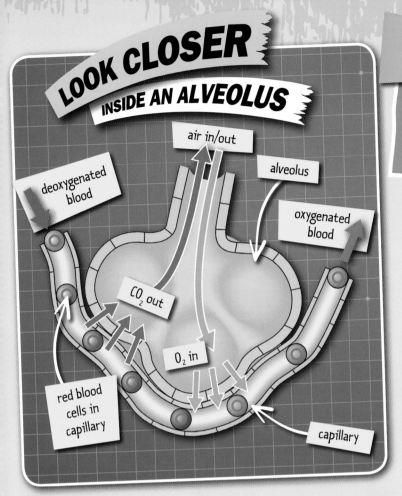

LOOK CLOSER
INSIDE AN ALVEOLUS

- air in/out
- alveolus
- deoxygenated blood
- oxygenated blood
- CO_2 out
- O_2 in
- red blood cells in capillary
- capillary

STRANGE BUT TRUE!

The word "lung" probably comes from an Old English word, "lunge." This meant "light"—as in, not weighing very much.

Exchanging gases

The alveolus's job is to deliver oxygen (O_2) to your blood. As you breathe in, the alveolus fills with air containing oxygen. As the blood moves along the capillaries, oxygen passes through the thin membrane, from the alveolus into the capillary. At the same time, a waste gas called carbon dioxide (CO_2) passes into the alveolus to be breathed out.

DON'T TRY THIS AT HOME!

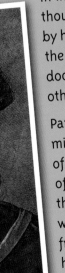

In the early 1500s, doctors thought sickness was caused by having too much of one of the four "humors." A German doctor called Paracelsus had other ideas.

Paracelsus noticed that miners often had sicknesses of their lungs—so he got hold of some dead miners, and cut them open to see what was wrong. It turned out that dust from the mines, not excessive humors, was causing the miners' sickness.

DID YOU KNOW?

Your blood can carry a LOT of oxygen.

Red blood cells contain a substance called **hemoglobin**. This substance carries oxygen around the body.

Each hemoglobin molecule can carry four oxygen molecules—and a SINGLE red blood cell contains about 250 million hemoglobin molecules. So in theory there could be a billion oxygen molecules on a single red blood cell!

OXYGEN DELIVERY, WASTE COLLECTION

As oxygen has been collected from the alveoli, it leaves your respiratory system and enters your circulatory system. From here it goes on a journey around the body, first to the heart and then on to where it is most needed.

Delivering and collecting

When the oxygen-rich blood leaves your lungs, it heads straight for your heart. From there, the blood is pumped out to the rest of your body through your circulatory system. Blood is first pumped into arteries that carry the oxygen-rich blood to the cells of your body.

When blood reaches a place in your body that needs oxygen, the tissue pulls the oxygen out of the blood through the thin capillary walls. The tissue might be part of a muscle, your brain, your liver or kidneys, your eyes, almost anywhere! As the oxygen is used, waste products are created, such as carbon dioxide.

LOOK CLOSER
CIRCULATORY SYSTEM

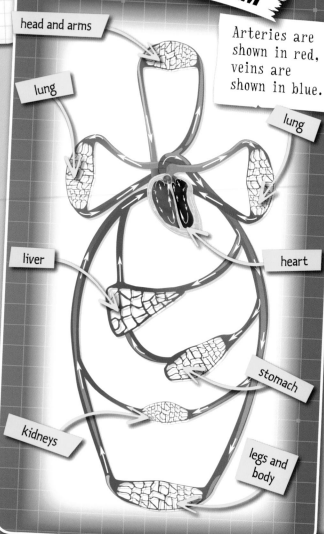

head and arms

lung

Arteries are shown in red, veins are shown in blue.

lung

liver

heart

stomach

kidneys

legs and body

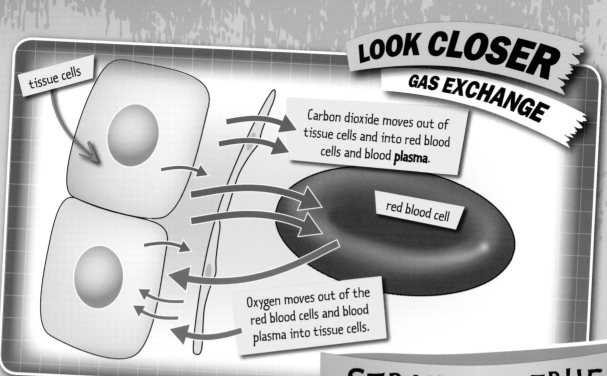

tissue cells

Carbon dioxide moves out of tissue cells and into red blood cells and blood **plasma**.

red blood cell

Oxygen moves out of the red blood cells and blood plasma into tissue cells.

Dangerous waste

Too much carbon dioxide is poisonous to humans, so your body needs to get rid of the excess as soon as possible! Your blood collects the carbon dioxide (there's room aboard, now that the oxygen has been delivered) and returns to the heart through your veins. The blood carries the carbon dioxide to your heart, which pumps it to your lungs. There, it rejoins the respiratory system: the carbon dioxide passes into the alveoli and is breathed out.

STRANGE BUT TRUE!

Many people breathe mainly through one nostril at a time. Their body changes nostrils regularly, and the change can happen after a few minutes or several hours. It has been claimed that which nostril you are mainly using has important effects. The right nostril is claimed to increase the level of glucose energy in your blood, and to draw in more oxygen than the left nostril.

DID YOU KNOW?

How freedivers breathe

You breathe to feed your body's need for oxygen, and to get rid of carbon dioxide.

Freedivers use special breathing techniques to lower the amount of carbon dioxide in their blood. This is what makes it possible for them to hold their breath for an amazingly long time.

BREATH CONTROL

You don't always breathe the same amount. Chasing your friend on a bicycle, for example, makes you breathe faster and harder than walking very slowly to math class. So how does your body know when, and how much, to breathe?

The brilliant brain stem

Your breathing is controlled by an area at the base of your brain called the brain stem. Your **nervous system** is constantly feeding it information about your blood vessels, muscles, and lungs. The brain stem uses this information to decide whether changes to your breathing are needed.

When you ride a bike fast, your muscles need extra energy. So that they get it, the brain stem sends a signal saying, "breathe faster." More breaths mean more oxygen reaching your lungs and blood. Your body uses this oxygen to provide your muscles with extra energy.

Exercise uses oxygen to burn fuel in your body for energy. A waste product is carbon dioxide, which is released into the blood. Your body needs to get rid of any excess carbon dioxide, since this can be poisonous.

① The body records high levels of carbon dioxide in the blood.

② The brain stem receives messages from the body.

③ The lungs are instructed to breathe harder.

④ Carbon dioxide is expelled and more oxygen is taken in.

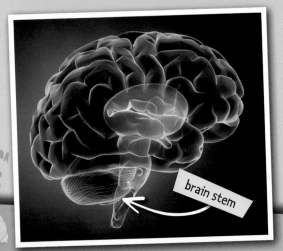

brain stem

Later, when you are walking to math class, your muscles need less energy than when you were racing on your bike. The brain stem tells your lungs it's okay to breathe more slowly.

Emotional breathing

Next time you watch a scary movie, stop and notice whether your breathing changes. It probably will! Your emotions affect your breathing. Feeling afraid or excited makes people breathe harder.

Experts think this is an old instinct from our early human ancestors. They would feel afraid when they saw something dangerous—a wolf or bear, perhaps. Their brain stems arranged an early delivery of oxygen, ready for running away or fighting.

See for yourself

You can easily see how your breathing changes according to what you are doing. Just count how many breaths you take in 30 seconds, while doing different activities. You could count breaths just before going to sleep, when walking to school, while running around, and while listening to relaxing music.

DID YOU KNOW?

Why you yawn?

Experts think yawning happens when the brain stem notices there are low oxygen levels in your blood. It triggers a yawn—which is just a way for your body to take in large amounts of oxygen quickly.

People mostly yawn when they are tired. Their body wants the extra burst of oxygen to provide a bit more energy. But people also yawn when they are scared. It's their brain's way of preparing the body to defend itself (or run away).

BREATHING— NOT THAT SIMPLE!

How do you breathe? You probably won't be able to answer that question without reading the rest of this page. That's because we all breathe automatically. This makes breathing seem simple— so it might surprise you to find out that it is actually quite complicated.

Breathing in air

Taking a breath starts with your **diaphragm**, a dome-shaped layer of muscle below your lungs. When you need to breathe in, your diaphragm shrinks downward and flattens out. This pulls the bottom of your lungs downward too. They expand and pull in air.

More muscles

The muscles between your ribs also help you breathe. They tighten and pull your rib cage upward and outward. This helps your lungs expand and draw in air. Finally, muscles in your stomach, and in your neck and shoulders, also swing into action when you take a breath. And all this happens between 15 and 60 times a minute!

LOOK CLOSER
BREATHING IN

Air is pulled into the lungs.

The lungs expand.

The diaphragm stretches flat and downward.

Your lungs are roughly cone shaped. The wide base is attached to your diaphragm.

16

Slippery lungs

To be able to pull in air, your lungs have to expand and deflate inside your chest. But how do they do this without rubbing against your rib cage? It's thanks to the **pleura**, a double membrane that surrounds each lung. One membrane is joined to the lung, the other to the chest cavity, and between them is a layer of fluid. This allows the outer layers to slide against each other, so the lung can easily inflate and deflate.

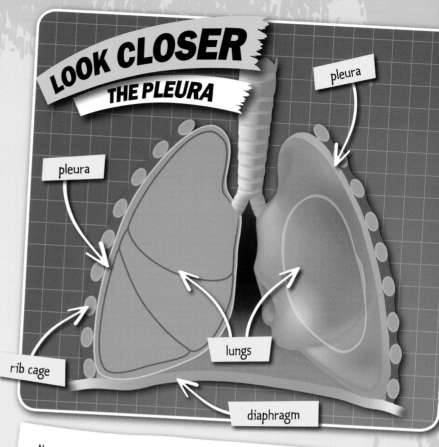

LOOK CLOSER
THE PLEURA

pleura

pleura

rib cage

lungs

diaphragm

DID YOU KNOW?

Hiccups are your diaphragm's fault.

Hiccups happen when your diaphragm suddenly tightens. This causes you to unexpectedly pull a lot of air into your lungs. Your body immediately wonders what's going on, and closes the gap in your **vocal cords** in case there's a problem. That's what makes the "hiccup" noise. In fact, hiccups are one of the few noises you can make when breathing in.

No one knows why hiccups happen, but lots of people think they know how to cure hiccups. Some crazy cures include:

✳ Hold your breath for as long as you can.

✳ Get somebody to scare you.

✳ Try sucking on a sour slice of lemon or eating a spoonful of sugar.

These "cures" probably won't work— but they will give anyone watching a good laugh.

HIC!

STRANGE BUT TRUE!

Charles Osborne of Iowa is said to be the record holder for hiccupping. He hiccupped nonstop for 68 years!

RELAX AND BREATHE OUT

How long can you hold your breath for? Most people can manage about 20 seconds. After that, your brain stem insists on getting rid of the excess carbon dioxide that has built up, and makes it impossible to hold your breath any longer. But how do you breathe out?

Diaphragm in command

Like breathing in, breathing out is controlled mainly by your diaphragm. The difference is that when you breathe out, your body doesn't have to do any work. The muscles in your diaphragm, rib cage, neck, and shoulders just relax. Everything goes back to its non-inflated position, and your lungs deflate, or get smaller. The air in the alveoli is pushed back out—through the bronchioles, then the bronchi, trachea, and finally your mouth or nose.

LOOK CLOSER
BREATHING OUT

Air is forced out through the trachea.

The lungs deflate.

The diaphragm relaxes and moves upward.

Breath temperature

By the time air has circulated through your lungs and been breathed out, it has been warmed (or cooled) by your body. You can easily check this for yourself. On an especially cold or hot day, hold your hand in front of your mouth and blow out. Can you feel a difference in temperature between your breath and the surrounding air?

The moisture in breath is visible in cold air.

Moisture in your breath

Your lungs have a moist atmosphere. As air circulates through them, it collects some of the moisture. In fact, the air picks up so much that adults lose about 17 ounces (0.5 L) of water from their body EVERY DAY—just by breathing out!

STRANGE BUT apparently TRUE!

In Tibet, monks trying to keep warm in the cold winter have developed something called g-tummo. They use special breathing and thinking techniques to raise their body temperatures by up to 33.8° F (1° C). Scientists are still not sure exactly how this works!

See for yourself

Make a fake lung!

1. Cut the base off a plastic bottle.

2. Tie a knot in a balloon, then cut across it at the widest part. Keep the knotted end and throw the other part away.

3. Stretch the wide, cut part of the balloon over the hole at the base of the bottle.

4. Put a straw into the neck of another balloon, and use an elastic band to keep it in place.

5. Push the balloon down through the neck of the bottle and keep the straw sticking out.

6. Seal the opening around the straw with modeling clay. (Make sure you haven't crushed the straw: air has to be able to get into the balloon.)

The balloon inside the bottle acts as a lung. The balloon stretched across the end of the bottle acts as the diaphragm. Pull down on the knot of the bottom balloon, then let it go back to a non-stretched position. What happens to the other balloon?

THE LUNG PROTECTION SQUAD

If your lungs stop working, you can die within minutes. Because of this, they need to be protected from damage. Your lungs aren't QUITE surrounded by body armor—that would make walking around very heavy work. But they do have a very effective equivalent.

Underneath the lungs

Your lungs are in an area of your body called the **thoracic cavity**. This area inside your chest contains your heart, lungs, and food pipe (**esophagus**). Below the thoracic cavity is your **abdominal cavity**. This contains your stomach, liver, kidneys, intestines, and other organs. Separating the two cavities is your diaphragm.

The amazing rib cage

Your rib cage is a set of bones that, together with your backbone and breastbone, surround your lungs. Flexible **cartilage** at the end of each rib links to a bone at the front of your chest—the **sternum**. The cartilage lets your ribs expand when you breathe in, and also allow the rib cage to act as a shock absorber, taking the force of dangerous blows. These blows either break ribs or tear the cartilage. This REALLY hurts—but it is much better than damaging your lungs.

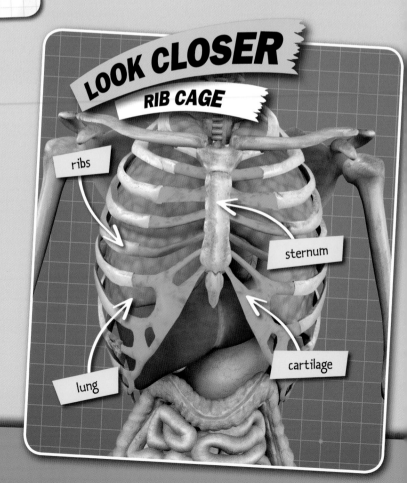

LOOK CLOSER

RIB CAGE

ribs

sternum

cartilage

lung

Your diaphragm stretches across the bottom of your rib cage. There are holes in it, which allow blood vessels, the esophagus, and nerves to pass through. Muscles connect your diaphragm to the walls of the thoracic cavity and to your spine.

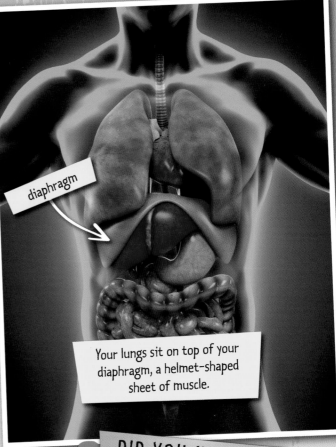

diaphragm

Your lungs sit on top of your diaphragm, a helmet-shaped sheet of muscle.

DON'T TRY THIS AT HOME!

In Victorian times, people who wanted a slimmer waist sometimes wore a device called a corset. It laced up like the top part of a shoe, and when the laces were pulled tight, they squeezed the waist. This pushed the lower ribs, diaphragm, and some digestive parts inward.

Even girls as young as 10 or 11 wore corsets. The idea was to "train" their waist to be thinner. The tight corsets prevented their bodies from growing naturally. Some women are even said to have ended up relying on them so much that they found it difficult to sit up without one.

DID YOU KNOW?

Elephants can go snorkeling!

Compared to most other animals, elephants have an extra layer of lung protection. Their lungs are surrounded by tough tissue that joins their lungs to their chest cavity. This strong structure prevents the lungs from being squashed by the pressure of deep water. Without it, an elephant's lungs could collapse if it swam underwater!

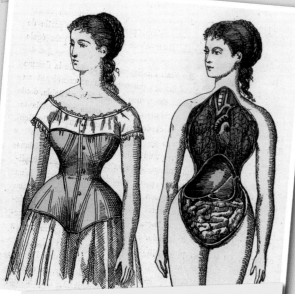

Corsets were popular back when no one knew what they did to your insides!

An elephant goes snorkeling.

21

WHAT'S IN A SNEEZE?

Normally, breathing out is just a question of relaxing. Not always, though! Sometimes, air leaves your lungs at high speed. When something causes your diaphragm to contract suddenly and powerfully, the muscles in your ribs do the same—and you sneeze.

What causes sneezes?

Sneezing has two main causes:

Expelling a foreign body

Sometimes, you breathe in an object that really doesn't belong up your nose. It might be **pollen** from a plant, dust, pepper, or just about anything else that you might breathe in. To expel the foreign body, your brain triggers a sneeze. This is why sneezes usually come in groups: your brain knows that one sneeze isn't usually enough to get rid of the intruder.

DID YOU KNOW?

Plucking your eyebrows can make you sneeze.

Plucking your eyebrows sometimes triggers a nerve that makes your brain think there's something up your nose. Your brain triggers a sneeze in an attempt to clear the obstruction—which was never actually there!

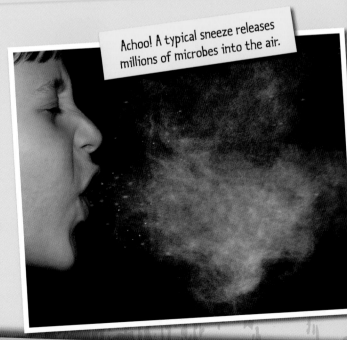

Achoo! A typical sneeze releases millions of microbes into the air.

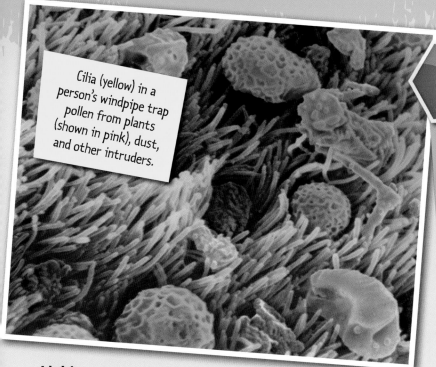

Cilia (yellow) in a person's windpipe trap pollen from plants (shown in pink), dust, and other intruders.

DON'T TRY THIS ON A RAINY DAY!

In 2010, a new species of monkey was discovered in the mountains of northern Myanmar. The monkeys have unusual nostrils, which point upward.

When questioned, local people said they had always known about the monkeys. They are hard to miss—especially on rainy days. Then, the monkeys are constantly sneezing because of water running into their upturned noses. Some even sit with their heads between their legs, in an attempt to stay dry!

Light

When some people move from dark into light, they sneeze. This is called a **photic sneeze**. Experts think it is caused by a mix-up between two nerves:

✳ The **trigeminal nerve**, which sends signals for a sneeze if a foreign body enters your nose.

✳ The **optic nerve**, which sends messages about light conditions.

These two nerves are very close together, and it seems likely that the signals they carry sometimes get mixed up.

How fast is a sneeze?

Lots of people claim that sneezes travel at 62 mph (100 kph), or even 99 mph (160 kph). There's no evidence that people actually do sneeze this fast. Recent studies have recorded people sneezing at six to 24 mph (10–39 kph). Even so, sneezing is a violent action. People sometimes damage muscles after a particularly violent sneeze—especially if they try to **suppress**, or stop, the sneeze.

Moving into bright light will cause your optic nerve to react quickly.

STRANGE BUT TRUE!

It's almost unheard of for people to sneeze in their sleep, and practically no one can sneeze with their eyes open. It is almost impossible to stop yourself sneezing, once a sneeze has begun.

WITHOUT LUNGS, YOU CAN'T TALK

Your lungs do more than just power your respiratory system (as if that's not enough!). They also make it possible for you to talk. You also need lungs for singing, whistling, whispering, and shouting.

BRILLIANT BODY FACT

Lung power can make the human voice louder than a jet engine!

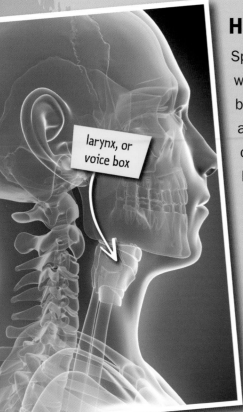

larynx, or voice box

How is speech made?

Speech comes from the **larynx**, which is also called the voice box. It's not actually a box at all. It's a complicated structure of cartilage and muscle. The larynx is at the top of the trachea, the tube leading from your throat down to your lungs.

Stretched across your larynx are two pieces of membrane. These are called the vocal cords. As air flows out of your lungs it passes between the vocal cords. While you are silent, the vocal cords are relaxed and open. When you want to speak, muscles around the larynx pull the cords tight and control the flow of air. The vocal cords vibrate as the air flows past, and this produces sounds.

The sounds your vocal cords produce are made clearer by your mouth, especially your tongue. To prove this to yourself, try speaking with your tongue pressed against the bottom of your mouth the whole time...

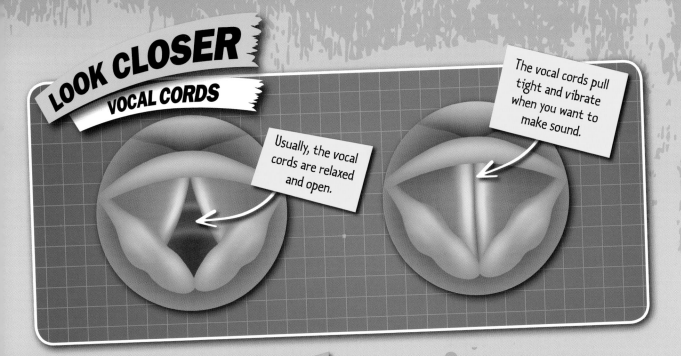

Usually, the vocal cords are relaxed and open.

The vocal cords pull tight and vibrate when you want to make sound.

STRANGE BUT TRUE!

No student will be surprised to hear that the world's loudest voice belongs to a teacher! Annalisa Flanagan, from Northern Ireland, was recorded shouting at 121.7 decibels—which is louder than a low-flying jet plane. Her twin sister is almost as loud, at 119 decibels!

DID YOU KNOW?

The vocal cords vibrate a LOT.

For example, to sing the note A above middle C vocal cords have to vibrate 440 times per second!

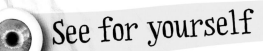 # See for yourself

The loudness of your voice depends on how much air is being expelled from your lungs. So does the length of time you can make the noise.

LOUDER = more air needed.

LONGER = more air needed.

To test this, try taking a deep breath before quietly saying the names of all the kids in your class. Then take another deep breath and try SHOUTING the names. Do you get as far?

LUNG TROUBLE

For normal, daily life, your lungs have far more capacity than you need. That's why even people with only ONE lung can still do most everyday activities (though they do run out of breath more quickly). Your respiratory system is not indestructible, though, and it can sometimes develop problems.

Asthma

Asthma is a medical condition that makes it hard to get enough air into your lungs. An asthma attack happens when your body reacts to a "trigger" by narrowing your airways. This makes it harder for air to reach your lungs. Common triggers include house dust, pollen, cigarette smoke, animal fur, and exercise.

Asthma cannot be cured, but knowing what is likely to trigger an attack makes it possible to control. If an attack does happen, medicine can help. Many people with asthma carry a **puffer** containing medicine that will open their airways.

LOOK CLOSER
ASTHMA

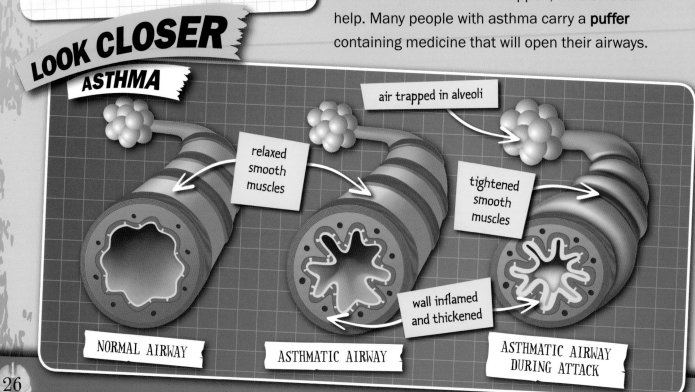

air trapped in alveoli

relaxed smooth muscles

tightened smooth muscles

wall inflamed and thickened

NORMAL AIRWAY

ASTHMATIC AIRWAY

ASTHMATIC AIRWAY DURING ATTACK

Pollution

Pollution is harmful material contained in the air, such as cigarette smoke or gases from vehicle exhaust. Your lungs can cope with a small amount of pollution. The cilia that line your airways move tiny particles of pollution out of the respiratory system. Too much pollution coats the cilia so much that they cannot expel it, and your lungs become clogged up.

Snot—fighting infection

If you've ever had a runny nose, you are familiar with one of the main ways your respiratory system defends itself against illness! The mucus, or snot, pouring out of your nose is part of your body's attempt to fight off a virus or bacteria. Viruses and bacteria can affect your airways. As the body tries to fight them off, it produces more mucus, which makes it harder to breathe or even stops your lungs from working properly.

A normal lung (left) and a lung damaged by smoking (right). Smoking allows harmful chemicals into your lungs, causing damage.

DID YOU KNOW?

The common cold really IS common.

More people catch the common cold every year than any other sickness of the respiratory system. It is the cause of the largest number of visits to the doctor, and the most missed days from school and work. Some experts think the common cold may be the commonest illness of ALL.

In many cities, some people wear face masks to keep out pollution and germs.

DON'T TRY THIS AT HOME!

Well, you could TRY these "cures" next time you have a cold. There's just no evidence that they would work.

Wrap your throat in dirty socks (England)
Make sure you grease the outside of your throat with chicken fat or lard, or the cure won't work. (Hint: it won't work anyway.)

Make yourself some lizard soup (Hong Kong, China)
Actually, this soup is not made using only dried lizards. It also contains yams and Chinese dates.

STRANGE BUT TRUE!

The bronchi in your lungs have taste buds, similar to the ones in your mouth. Researchers have found that bitter tastes cause the lungs to relax. This knowledge may one day be used to treat asthma.

MAINTENANCE AND SERVICING

BRILLIANT BODY FACT

Playing a wind instrument helps your lungs to work better!

Everything you do depends on your body getting oxygen. If your lungs do not work properly, you may not always get enough oxygen. Things that you think about—like maths tests—and those that you don't—like growing fingernails—would all become much harder. So, how can you keep your lungs in tip-top shape?

① Don't smoke, or be around smoke

Cigarette smoke, whether it comes from a cigarette you are smoking or someone else's, is very harmful to your lungs and respiratory system. Find out more on page 27.

② Campaign for clean air

Air pollution has similar harmful effects to smoking. Encourage politicians and other leaders to fight for clean air and you will help everyone's lungs, not only your own.

③ Run around!

Regular exercise is probably the best thing you can do for your lungs. Exercise makes your lungs breathe harder. The muscles you use to breathe get stronger and more flexible. Your lungs get better at exchanging carbon dioxide for oxygen. You also increase the amount of air your lungs can take in with a single breath.

As well as all these benefits, exercise makes your body better at using the oxygen your lungs provide. Your heart gets stronger and able to pump faster. Your blood vessels deliver the oxygen better. Exercise may even make you

Exercise is good for your lungs.

smarter: experts have shown that kids who exercise more soon also get better marks at school.

④ Avoid indoor pollution

Avoid indoor air pollution. This can come from wood and coal fires, **pet dander**, or even mold on walls or food. Keeping the indoors clean and well ventilated will reduce the risks.

⑤ Eat lung-loving foods

Surprisingly, research has shown that some foods are good for your lungs. In particular, people who eat plenty of broccoli, cauliflower, cabbage, pak choi, kale, and similar vegetables are less likely to get lung cancer.

Pet hair and dander can irritate some people's airways.

STRANGE BUT TRUE!

Playing a wind instrument can help asthma sufferers control their condition by making their lungs stronger. In fact, in Australia some asthma sufferers have been taught to play the **didgeridoo**, as part of their treatment!

A balanced diet includes plenty of fruits and vegetables.

DID YOU KNOW?

Lung is a popular meal.

Not human lung, obviously! But many of the animals we eat have lungs, and around the world they are a popular food. In Greece, lamb lungs are used to make soup for Easter; in Asia, they are cut into strips and fried. In the United States though, you can't eat lungs—it's illegal.

The most famous lung dish is Scottish haggis. Traditionally, this is made from the heart and lungs of a lamb, mixed with other ingredients, and tied up inside a sheep's stomach before being cooked. It tastes better than it sounds or looks!

BREATHTAKING WORDS!

Note: Some boldfaced words are defined where they appear in the book.

abdominal cavity An area of your body between your chest and hips, which contains your stomach, liver, kidneys, intestines, and other organs

airways Passages that allow air to travel to and from your lungs

blood vessels The tubes carrying blood around your body

capillaries The smallest type of blood vessels, with walls so thin that gases and some chemicals can pass through

carbon dioxide A gas that in excess is poisonous to humans. Its chemical formula is CO_2.

cartilage Tough tissue that connects parts of the human body, in particular bones

didgeridoo A hollow wooden tube played as a musical instrument

esophagus The pipe that you swallow food down. It leads from the throat to the stomach.

freediver A person who swims in deep water, without using scuba diving equipment that would allow him or her to breathe below the surface

hemoglobin A protein found in blood that transports oxygen

lobe A curved or rounded part of an organ

membrane Very thin tissue

microbe A microorganism that exists as just one cell, and can only be seen with a microscope

mucus A slimy substance produced by the body that traps dirt and microbes. It also lubricates some parts of the body.

nasal passages The airways that connect your nostrils to your throat

nervous system The body system made up of nerve cels through which the brain sends and receives information about what is happening in the body and around it

oxygen A colorless gas that is present in the air. Humans breathe in air and use the oxygen to release energy from food.

pet dander Dead skin that has flaked off and then been trapped in the fur of a pet animal

plasma The fluid part of blood

pollen Tiny, powdery grains that are released by plants

puffer A device carried by people who have asthma. A puffer contains chemicals that are breathed into the lungs and help the person to breathe normally.

thoracic cavity The area inside your chest, protected by your ribs, which contains your heart, lungs, and esophagus

vocal cords The structures at the top of your trachea, which change shape when air moves across them, allowing you to make different sounds

BREATHLESS INFORMATION

Are you gasping for more information? Here are some good places to find out more about the lungs and respiratory system:

BOOKS TO READ

Burnstein, John. *The Remarkable Respiratory System: How do my lungs work?* Crabtree Publishing, 2009.

Claybourne, Anna. Smelly Farts and Other Body Horrors. Crabtree Publishing, 2015.

Rooney, Anne. *A Math Journey Through the Human Body.* Crabtree Publishing, 2015.

Shea, John. *The Respiratory System.* Gareth Stevens, 2012.

WEBSITES

http://kidshealth.org/kid/htbw/lungs.html

This website is a great place to find out all sorts of information about the human body. It has an excellent section on the respiratory system.

www.neok12.com/Respiratory-System.htm

This website has all sorts of information for kids on how the respiratory system works, including diagrams, videos, and quizzes.

PLACES TO VISIT

In Boston, Massachusetts, the Hall of Human Life at the **Museum of Science** has over 70 interactive exhibits about how the body works. The museum is located at:

Museum of Science
1 Science Park
Boston, MA 02114
www.mos.org

The **Museum of Science and Industry** in Chicago, Illinois, features YOU! The Experience, a permanent exhibition celebrating human life. The museum is located at:

The Museum of Science and Industry
5700 S. Lake Shore Drive
Chicago, IL 60637
www.msichicago.org

In Columbus, Ohio, the **Center of Science and Industry** explores the human body in their exhibition Life: The Story of You. The museum is located at:

Center for Science and Industry
333 W. Broad Street
Columbus, OH 43215
www.cosi.org

INDEX

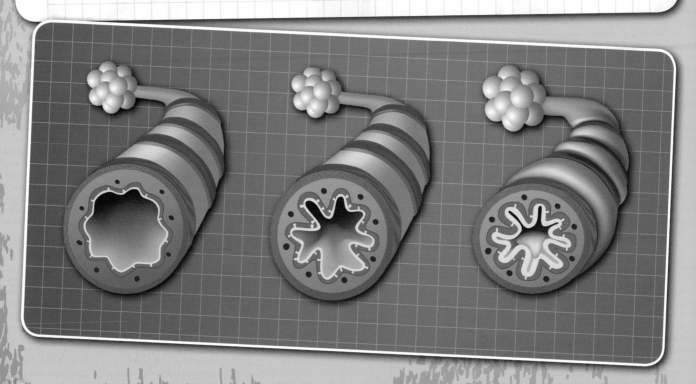